MW01289716

Putting the
YOU
in Recruiting

Putting the YOU in Recruting:

A Step-by-Step Process for Attracting and Acquiring Talent

Yoselyn Hollow
with Kevin Pierce

CONTENTS

LOOKING BACK

I met Yoselyn as a referral.

For a writer, referrals are a mixed bag. A friend or client knows someone who'd be perfect to write a book with.

Oh boy.

But this referral came from a relative, so I couldn't just blow it off.

She met me in the RE/MAX lobby and showed me to her office, where I noticed that the J-sound "Jocelyn" I was meeting spelled the name on her door with a "Y." I asked her for the correct pronunciation.

"The 'J' sound is right," she said. "The "Y" spelling is a Latina thing. It's kind of a hook."

Oh boy. Kind of a hook. Just the kind of thing great business books are always based on.

We spent some time talking about the writing process and how technology was changing the publishing business.

Then I asked what kind of a story she might tell in a book:

1

How to Sell Your Home in the New Economy? How to Stage Your Home for a Quick Sale?

This time, it was her turn with the "Oh Boy" moment...

"Do you know how many houses I've sold in seven years?" she asked.

Not knowing there would be a test, I had absolutely no clue what a successful real estate agent might sell. Maybe five or ten properties a month? Fifty or 100 a year? Several hundred over the course of several years?

"I've sold exactly two," she said. "And only because I owned them." She told me her success in real estate had come from something completely different: recruiting.

"And that," she said, "is what I do."

And that was when she had me hooked.

Over the next many weeks, Yoselyn would explain how she became one of the most successful real estate recruiters in the nation, the systems she developed for recruiting agents and her tips for broker/owners or recruiters interested in emulating her success.

As I thought back to my previous career in broadcast management, I realized Yoselyn's recruiting systems would have served me well. And with minor adaptation, they could benefit any enterprise with a sales staff.

It is my pleasure to introduce to you to Yoselyn. With a "J" sound.

It might be a hook, but it's one she doesn't need.

Oh boy.

Kevin Pierce
Fort Myers, FL

WELCOME TO THE BIG BACKYARD

I was born and raised in Boston. My mother is from Costa Rica and moved to Massachusetts when she was fifteen. My dad is from Puerto Rico and lived in Chicago before moving to Boston. My father is eight years older than my mother; they met when my mom was 17, got married and had me a year and a week later.

My brother came along four years after that, and we lived in an apartment building in Chelsea, Massachusetts.

We have a very large family on both sides, and I was fortunate to grow up with my cousins, my aunts and my uncles all nearby. One aunt and uncle owned the apartment building to the left of us, we lived in ours, and another aunt and uncle owned the building to the right, so we were like in a big circle with all of our backyards connected. It was one giant backyard where all of us were able to play and just be together. We called it "El Patio." We were our own community.

Because we had each other, there was practically no need for any of us to have other friends. So we grew up together and as a result, we are still very, very close.

Even when I first married and moved away, every weekend we would still go back to El Patio.

It was the best childhood. When I speak with my cousins – we don't see each other very often now – it's almost like life goes right back to when we were kids.

I think almost unconsciously, I've tried to bring a little of El Patio to my business. I recruit agents who seem like they'll fit "the family," and avoid those who won't. Just like the different ages of my cousins, we always have agents with a mix of experience levels – and the learning goes in both directions.

As you prepare to grow your business by recruiting, you'll need to spend some time thinking about the business you want to become.

By thinking through this process in advance of your growth and recruiting efforts, you can design a big backyard of your own.

Questions for YOU:

◆ As you consider the kind of business you'd like yours to become, how is that vision different from what you have today?

◆ What types of people will you choose to work with? What types will you avoid?

◆ What attitudes and sensibilities will you desire in future team members? Which ones will you avoid?

A MOTHER'S SECRETS

My mother turns out to be very good at keeping secrets. You should be pretty good at it, too.

I was living in an apartment in Boston. I had only been dating Michael for a short time. We had been best friends for years before becoming romantic, so we had a strong foundation.

Strong enough that we decided to buy a house together.

Michael and I looked, narrowed down our home choices and made an offer. We were just waiting for approval of the loan commitment from the bank.

The new house had hardwood floors. It was a colonial, two-story, attic and basement and it had wood floors everywhere. Michael's place was all carpeted, so he never owned a pair of slippers. What better way to tell him that we finally got the loan commitment than to give him a pair of slippers and say congratulations on our new home?

I swore my mother to silence and told her of my slipper plans. She went to work.

Michael's family is Irish. And St. Patrick's Day was coming. So my Spanish mother announced a St. Patrick's Day dinner. Corned beef and cabbage? None of us had ever had it. Even to this day, I've never had corned beef and cabbage. It just doesn't sound good.

Not only was she cooking Irish food, but she also invited everybody in my family: very Spanish and very big. I have 13 aunts and uncles on my mother's side, almost that many on my father's side, plus 15 or so cousins.

The loan approval came, so I went out and got Michael's slippers and a card. I had everything wrapped up and ready. My mother liked Michael and was excited to hear that we were approved for the financing. I told her we could start buying stuff for the house.

So, on St. Patrick's Day, my mother served two dishes, the corned beef and cabbage plus something else for everybody who wouldn't eat it. Michael and I were in the dining room, and I saw my mother ushering in the rest of the family. She gave me a nod, but before I could reach for my gift, Michael got on one knee and said, "You're my best friend. I want to spend the rest of my life with you. Will you marry me?" He put a ring on my finger, we hugged and kissed and everybody was happy.

Then, it was my turn. "Wait, I've got something for you." I said. He opened the package and looked at the slippers, and it dawned on him. "We've got the house?" he asked. I told him that we did.

And we also had a mother (and soon-to-be mother-in-law) who could keep two secrets at the same time. Turns out that Michael had gone to her with his plans to propose and she suggested that it should happen at a St. Patrick's Day dinner she was planning – a dinner that already had one secret associated with it.

In business, we're frequently asked to keep confidential many things we learn or hear. Unfortunately, many disregard this simple request and do damage to the person who shared the information, as well as harm their own reputation in the process.

Learn to keep a confidence. You might gain a son-in-law or help your daughter celebrate the start of a new life. At the very worst, you might get a new pair of slippers.

Questions for YOU:

◆ How might you make use of confidential information without violating a trust?

◆ How might keeping a secret benefit your image with your team? With potential recruits?

◆ Under what circumstances (if any) would you violate a confidence?

TRUSTING OTHERS' DECISIONS

Michael, has always hated the cold. It didn't bother me because it was all I had ever known. But Michael had come to Florida several times as a young boy, so he knew of a warmer place. Years after we were married, one winter day, he announced that he was going to start looking into jobs in Florida.

We were settled in with a son in middle school and a newborn daughter; I didn't think anything would come of it.

I was wrong.

Over the years, Michael made several golfing trips to Florida, and continued to plant seeds with me about an eventual move. After our daughter was born, we made plans to come down with the kids to visit his parents at their Florida home.

We did the whole tourist thing: Walt Disney World with the kids and a stop in Southwest Florida to visit his mother and father. He was still going on and on about moving here, and I finally just looked at him and said, "Stop. Whatever it is that you want to do, just do it. But stop talking to me about it and get it done." I really expected him to drop the whole thing, but Michael took me very literally. He started applying for jobs.

When we got back to Boston, we talked about putting the house on the market. I had worked for a real estate company, so we called an agent there – we had bought the house through her. I was still certain that nothing was going to happen; I didn't think that we would be able to get what we needed out of it.

I said, "Fine. Go ahead with it. Put the sign on the property."

At the same time, Michael got a call from a sheriff's office in Florida. They were interested in hiring him, but he would need a couple of weeks of training. So he took off for Florida, leaving me with two kids and a house for sale.

It was on the market for a week, and we got a full price offer.

The phone call to Michael about the offer didn't go over so well because I was hysterical, crying. I said, "Maybe we priced it too low, maybe I can ask for a little bit more." But he said, "No, we are doing this." And then my panic really set in, because I really wasn't ready to move to Florida. We were selling our house. Where would I live? What would become of our things? He tried to reassure me over the phone, but it wasn't the same as having him here.

We accepted the offer.

Michael came back from training and over the next several weeks, we packed up the house – all four floors of it. The kids and I moved in with my parents, and Michael left again to start his new job in Florida.

When it was time for us to join Michael, it would be in a new house he had found, but that I only knew through pictures. I told him right before we left for Florida, "Either I'm going to love you, or I'm going to hate you." We are still happily married so, obviously, he was very wise with his house selection.

All these huge life changes – deciding to move to Florida, selling our first house, buying a new one – were possible only because I trusted Michael to chart a path that would be good for our family. The decisions weren't mine; trusting Michael was.

The same kinds of situations can present themselves in business. An employee who has earned your trust sees a market opportunity that could be good for the agency. Will you let him pursue it? A trusted team feels that pursuing a new category of business could be a long-term success. Will you encourage their effort?

Letting go – and letting someone else follow a passion that aligns with your goals – is never easy. But it might be the best way to acknowledge your trust.

It can definitely get you to a warmer winter.

Questions for YOU:

◆ If an agent who has earned your trust wanted to pursue a new market (bank-owned properties or short sales, perhaps), what limits would you place on the effort?

◆ If a trusted agent proposed a new system for lead generation, how much freedom would you give? What, if any, restrictions would you insist on?

◆ In what ways could you demonstrate the trust you have in a team member, while keeping a limit on an untested idea?

GET STARTED, SOMEHOW

We moved into our new Florida home and I became a mommy-homemaker. That was one of the things I told Michael before we moved down (after I realized that I wasn't going to get out of the move): I have a newborn baby, and I don't want to work. I had been fortunate enough to stay home with our son for his first three years, and I had every intention of doing the same with our daughter.

That lasted a month.

It was Christmas, and the holidays were very hard for me. One thing that I had always known – the big family Christmas – was gone. And it was hard to get into the holiday spirit in warm weather, wearing flip flops and a tank top.

And I was bored. There is only so much cleaning that you can do to a house, and I got to the point that dinner was ready by noon. I couldn't pick up the phone and call someone because I didn't know anybody here, and everybody I knew back home was working.

Plus, I was used to making my own money and being self-sufficient. If I wanted to go out and buy something or do something, I could. But with my husband as the only breadwinner, I really couldn't. That was the deciding factor.

Michael and I talked about a part-time job that would get me out of the house and let me interact with other people – adults, people who would actually talk back.

One of the things that I enjoyed the most working in Boston was my job in real estate. So I got out the Yellow Pages and called three different companies in Cape Coral. Two of them were Century 21; the third was this RE/MAX office. I left messages for all three in a voicemail resume: This is where I worked, these are my references, this is what I can do, this is what I have done, I'm bilingual, please call me.

This office was the only one to call me back, only to say there was nothing available. I asked that they keep my contact information in case something changed or in case they ran into other brokers looking to bring somebody on. I told them it didn't have to be a management position, I just wanted to work.

They called again the next morning. A front desk administrator was leaving. They said they knew it wasn't what I was looking for. What they didn't know was that I would have cleaned bathrooms.

We scheduled an interview.

I met with the office manager. We were going through the basics. Midway through, he phoned the broker/owner and said, "You need to meet this woman."

The broker/owner came right over and looked at my resume. He noted I was a recruiter, and asked how many people I brought on. I had no idea. My old company had grown, but, I told him, I never counted heads.

He asked when I could start. I said tomorrow or whenever you want. So we picked a day and I left. We never even talked about pay, and I didn't care. And I think they knew that. Whether they saw promise in me, or dedication, or loyalty, or just the need and the desire to be a part of something, I don't know. But they offered me the position and I took it.

I am a firm believer that things always happen for a reason, that you are destined to do whatever it is that you do, and things fall in place just the way they are supposed to (or don't fall into place because they're not supposed to).

I might not understand the reason when it's happening – or even ever – but this was my role, this is what I was destined to do.

Questions for YOU:

◆ What areas of your responsibilities could use a "jump start"?

◆ What low-risk effort could you make a start on today? This week?

◆ What back-burner ideas could your team get started on to prove or disprove its viability?

HOLD THE PHONE

The first thing I noticed about answering phones in Cape Coral, Florida, was how difficult it was for me to understand people from Florida.

To a Spanish-speaker from Boston, Floridians have the thickest, most southern accent. I would answer the phone and have somebody on the other end that, for the life of me, I couldn't understand. I would apologize and ask that they repeat themselves. But there were only so many times I could do that before I would run the risk of ticking them off. So I'd put them on hold and let the other administrator take the information because I couldn't.

Lots of times, callers couldn't understand me, either. What the hell, is that English? Is that Spanish? What are you saying? So that took a lot of getting used to. After a while, though, I started understanding more, and – by speaking slowly – was able to make myself understood.

But the most important thing was that by answering the phone, I got to meet all of the agents in the area. They were always calling about our listings and to arrange showings.

I knew what would be expected of me in terms of growing the company (already thinking about my next job here). What an opportunity! The people I'll need to meet with and recruit are ringing my phone every day.

The more often the same agent might call, the more questions I would ask while we were on the phone. I would establish a rapport with them, a relationship over the phone.

That's how I got my first recruiting appointment. I was talking to an agent and I asked her to come into the office and give me a few minutes of her time.

Was I ready to make a presentation? Not anywhere close. But I had an appointment and I was going to make her my first recruit.

Questions for YOU:

♦ What existing contacts and conduits provide a stream of potential recruits to or through your office?

♦ How can you make more frequent contact with potential recruits?

♦ How can you establish a rapport with the potential recruits who interact with your office?

FIRST RECRUIT

I t was a big advantage for me to start at the front desk because I was able to talk to a lot of agents that were calling. I was able to see who was active and who had a good book of business.

I requested access to the multiple listing service, so after I talked to these people on the phone, I could do a little bit of research and find out a bit about them, or at least see their picture on the MLS and put a face with the name.

As I got to know an agent, I'd always note when they showed another of our listings, pointing out to them that if they were over here, they wouldn't have to call all the time. I'd throw that out there to see if they'd bite.

That's how I got my first recruiting appointment. This agent was calling on a regular basis to show our listings. I told her, maybe she should be at RE/MAX. And she took me up on it.

I was scared and nervous. I had my first person actually bite. What was I going to say? What was I going to do?

I was brand new and didn't know anything about selling RE/MAX or the office. So I asked the office manager if he would do the interview for me, letting me watch and learn. He agreed.

This was important for me because in Boston, I had worked at Century 21 and recruited against RE/MAX. I always told agents they didn't want to go to RE/MAX because RE/MAX would charge them for everything. You want to make a photocopy? You pay for it. You want a paperclip? You pay for it. You want a stapler? You pay for it. And then, I'd tell them that in my Century 21 office you don't pay for anything. We are just going to put you on a standard split and you won't pay a thing. As long as they didn't question the "standard split," that worked great. Unlike RE/MAX, everything was "included."

What they weren't seeing was that with a commission split of 50-50, 60-40 or even 70-30, there is still a portion of what you earn in commission that stays in the office. So a $100,000 producer on a 70-30 means that $30,000 stays on the table. They've thrown $30,000 toward paperclips, staplers and copies, but they think they don't pay for anything.

I wanted to see the office manager's technique for explaining this and what he did to deal with the misconception. But I quickly realized that he thought it was all about RE/MAX and what we do. He was vomiting RE/MAX.

At one point, he brought out a white board and was just writing down the costs and the numbers. All the talk about expenses was making me uncomfortable; I could only imagine how the candidate was feeling.

Remember, she was coming from one of those companies

where she didn't pay anything. In her mind, she didn't pay for signs, writers, copies, long distance, office space... What we should've been explaining is that her $30,000 split is what she paid, whether she used it or not. We should've been pointing out how much that really cost. This was her business, and she should know exactly what her annual expenses and fixed expenses were going to be. She should be able to budget for that.

I needed to figure out a way to identify what a candidate's expenses were, so that we could compare apples to apples against their old companies, and show a value to the way we do it. That was something that he did very, very poorly.

I realized that this was not the way that I wanted to conduct interviews. I didn't know then how I was going to do it; I just knew that this was not the way.

We did win this agent and signed her up, but it would be the last time I would bring the office manager in on one of my interviews.

Questions for YOU:

◆ What misperceptions might potential recruits have about their existing offices?

◆ What misperceptions might they have about your office?

◆ What aspect of your office is most difficult to explain to a candidate? How could you change the perception of this feature?

29

REACHING FOR
THE MIDDLE

As I began my recruiting for RE/MAX, I knew I would need to target agents that I would focus a recruiting effort on. But as I was new to the area and new to the office, I really didn't have a personal knowledge of who they should be.

I started asking for help in the form of referrals. Any time I was interviewing a prospect, or a new agent came aboard, I asked them who they would recommend from their former office.

I would ask if they knew somebody who was going through the same things as they were, facing the same challenges and uncertainties, and whether I could give that person a call and tell them where I got their name. Sometimes even before I'd ask for a referral, a prospect or new agent would mention some names in their office. I would always tune in and keep them in the back of my mind.

Before I started getting the referrals, I would just go into the MLS and do a search. Who were the top 20, 30, 40 agents in a given office?

But I realized that the top producers should not be my hit list target. I would look for the middle producers, instead.

Often the middle agents are the forgotten ones. Most brokers and managers will spend a lot of time with the top producers. With these prima donnas, the egos are a lot bigger, so managers make sure they're taken care and comfortable, and that everything is hunky dory with them.

Brokers also have to spend time with new agents coming on board. It takes a lot to get the part- timers or the new agents up and running. They need help with all the systems, constant hand holding and cheerleading.

With all the attention on the top and bottom, managers neglect the middle. But the middle producers are the ones who are consistent. They're the ones who come in and do their work, have a good book of business, and have their systems already in place. Their soon-to-be-former broker wonders why he would need to spend time talking with them to see how they're doing? So the middle producers were forgotten.

And that's who I targeted.

I would run an office's production numbers and take a look at who was doing what. I skipped over the top producers and the ones that were doing less than a million dollars or just started.

I concentrated on the middle producers and it paid off. I was able to spend the time with them that their current broker wasn't, giving the 'atta boys and the 'atta girls and the recognition they wanted and deserved. I let them know I noticed when they closed on a deal. I'd congratulate them for earning one of their designations. I'd point out that I'd seen the great ad they ran in the paper. I was doing everything their own broker wasn't.

I was determined to essentially be their broker before I actually became their broker. I knew people would want to work with me if they liked me and respected me. I wanted to be a magnet that would attract agents to do business with me because they knew I genuinely cared and was sincere.

This focus on the middle doesn't mean that we ignored top producers completely. But I have found that they are pretty set. Unless something catastrophic happens in their office or with their broker, top producers are not likely to move. Many have been in place eight to ten years. I do put my feelers out and let them know I'm interested. I have recruited many agents that were top producers in other offices and subsequently closed a lot of offices as a result.

But most agents consider their first move after about a year and a half into the business. That's when they're middle producers – the heart of the office. That's when they're starting to produce and their pipeline is full. They project that they are going to do better next year than this year, so they are more likely to consider a move.

Another office's middle is a great place to be.

Questions for YOU:

◆ How might a focus on middle producers benefit your office?

◆ What volume amounts would describe the "middle producers" in your market?

◆ Are you paying enough attention to the middle producers in your office?

THE HIT LIST

I keep a hit list of agents that I plan to recruit to my office. The first thing I look for is their production level. But just as important is their personality. Production can get an agent onto the list, but their personality might get them off of it. Do we share the commitment and values that are so important to the success of the office?

Having someone in the office with a bad attitude is like having a vampire on board. When you see them coming, you want to run the other way because you know they will suck up all your energy and leave you drained. Life is way too short to be surrounded by people that you don't want to be around. I want to be among people who are happy and positive like I am.

I go to the MLS to check their production level, then pick up the phone to start a dialog with them. It's the combination that helps me decide whether they stay on the list.

I tweak my list on a regular basis. I have A, B, C and D as categories by production. Once a year I contact everyone to check that their addresses are current and review their production levels. Someone who used to be $1 million dollar producer and is now a $3 million dollar producer moves up to my B category; a one-time $4 million dollar producer who has dipped to $1 million drops to C. Agents who aren't doing anything – not at the benchmark where I think they should be in terms of minimum standards – are bumped off the list. And if I find they have a bad attitude – whether I experience it personally or hear about it from another agent – I don't care what their production level is, I am not asking them to come to my office, so I'm not keeping them on my list.

I keep 150 people on my hit list. Every time I successfully recruit one of them, I replace them with a new name.

If you're just setting up a list, the exact number of prospects isn't important. But you should be careful about adding too many. I've talked with people who have 500 or 1,000 names. That's not a list of potential recruits; that's a list of people who work in real estate. You have to keep it manageable, because you have to work the list.

By researching a prospect's production level and finding a reason to speak with them on the phone, I have interviewed them even before they realize that I am interviewing them. This lets me be selective with my list. Not everybody is good for my office and my office certainly isn't for everyone.

This vetting process is important because I don't want a revolving door. I want to identify people who will make a good business here and retire here.

Questions for YOU:

◆ How large a hit list can you realistically manage?

◆ What production levels would put a candidate on your hit list?

◆ What other factors might identify candidates for your hit list?

WHITE LIES

I cannot tell a lie; I got started by telling one (with apologies to George Washington).

I knew that I needed to schedule some recruiting interviews. And to do that, I'd need to make some phone calls. But I was new to town and didn't really know anybody, and didn't really know what to talk to anybody about.

So I lied.

I needed to be able to tell people I had a reason for calling them and to have something to talk about on the call. Something to talk about was pretty easy because of the universal issues in real estate: leads, commissions, structure, income, work environment, support, etc. Those are things that agents are always looking for.

The reason for calling was where the truth got stretched:

"Hi, it's Yoselyn with RE/MAX Realty Team. I interviewed one of your colleagues yesterday and they were talking about some frustrations with the lead generation systems in your office. Before they left, I asked if anybody else in their office might be interested in learning about our systems and what we have to offer. They gave me your name and your phone number."

Had I interviewed one of this agent's colleagues? No. Had anyone referred me to this agent? No. And I had looked up the contact information

Nine times out of ten, the agents found my call flattering. Sometimes, they'd ask who it was that referred them. Was it Bill, Sheila or Terry? I'd explain that I needed to keep the agent's confidence (as I wrote down Bill, Sheila and Terry as my next prospects).

I've had some people try to rationalize this for me as a "white lie," or a mistruth with no consequence, much like, "You look like you've lost weight," or "I like your hair."

I told this story as a presenter on a panel of brokers and owners for a real estate webinar. One person in the audience was really bothered by the fact that I had lied.

The moderator smoothed things over by pointing out that, by now, I had likely interviewed multiple agents from every office in my area, so that the part about "interviewing someone from your office," had actually become true on its own.

Questions for YOU:

◆ Could you tell a recruit a "white lie" if there was no consequence in doing so?

◆ What might you learn during an interview with one agent that might help interview others?

◆ What might be on your list of "universal reasons" for a call?

BE THEIR BROKER BEFORE YOU'RE THEIR BROKER

As you have contact with agents you'd like to be the broker for, try to become their broker before you're their broker.

When an agent is on your team, you let them know you care about their business, their well-being, their present and future production. You share ideas with them so they can be better agents. That's what's being a broker is all about. It means helping agents develop their business in the most efficient way possible.

As a recruiter, you need to demonstrate those broker-abilities to agents who have not (yet) joined your team.

In order for an agent to join and do business with you, they have to like you and respect you. This is a relationship that develops over time. Showing you're sincerely interested in developing their business – before they've decided to join your office – goes a long way toward growing those feelings.

Maybe there's an agent who has resisted a meeting with me. I can appeal to them with information to help their business.

When a new regulation was enacted last year for short sales, the agents on my hit list were unlikely to learn about it from their current brokers. So after sharing news about it with my existing agents, I told the agents I wanted on my team about it.

"Hi Jane. You know I hope you'll join my office someday. But I know that the timing isn't right for you, so I'm not going to ask you today. At the same time, I don't want you to find yourself in trouble. So I want to make sure you know about this new regulation and what it means to you so you can make sure you're prepared and protected."

That's all I say and that's all I do. Just what a broker should do. Even though I'm not their broker. Yet.

I'm always on the lookout for agents' accomplishments. Most brokers don't acknowledge these as often as they should. So whether it's production, professional development or a personal achievement, I give them a call. I let them know I noticed they were in a class, or earned a designation or hit some level of production. I tell them I hope it helps in their business and that I think they're doing a great job.

This gives me another reason to make a call where there's no pressure. It's just a sincere 'atta boy or 'atta girl. And it likely fills a void their existing broker/owner both created and failed to recognize.

A lot of agents will tell you they don't want the recognition.

That's crap. They do. They've accomplished something. Something important. They're proud of it, otherwise they wouldn't bother doing it. Everybody wants recognition, at least a small level of it.

There are many non-intrusive ways to approach an agent you're actively recruiting. It's all about strategically positioning yourself so that when there's a choice to be made, you're the one they choose. And showing them the kind of broker you'll be – when you're their broker – makes that choice even easier for them to make.

Questions for YOU:

◆ Where might you watch for accomplishments of the agents on your hit list?

◆ What business help might you offer to agents on your hit list?

◆ What are other ways you might play the role of an agent's broker before you're given the part?

CAPTURE THE KING

Recruiting is like a game of chess.

Every office in every market is staffed with pawns, bishops and knights, rooks, queens and kings. They represent all the staff jobs and agents that make an office run smoothly and profitably.

As you consider your own team a chess set, you need to identify what role your pieces will play. Recruiting should not be solely the role of the broker/owner or recruiter; it needs to be something that everybody in the office plays a part in, from the front desk all the way to the top agents. You need to utilize all your resources to help you attract agents into your workplace.

While the object of chess is to capture the other side's king, many pieces and many moves must work in and be made in concert toward that goal.

Chess is a strategic game, a combination of knowing your opponent's next move, anticipating it and understanding when to strike. Recruiting is no different.

To capture the other side's king requires that all your pieces do what's expected of them, when it's expected of them.

Questions for YOU:

◆ What roles do your office staff play in recruiting efforts?

◆ Are your staff members aware of the roles they play?

◆ Are their new or additional roles that should be assigned or developed?

UNIQUE OPPORTUNITY

The first step in recruiting is to recognize your office's unique opportunities.

Every one of us have desirable things – opportunities – in our offices. But it's not enough that they're opportunities; they must also be unique – something your office has that your competition does not. "I'm a great broker" or "I'm a great owner" isn't going to cut it. While it might be true, another office can have a great broker or great owner, too.

"We have No. 1 market share" is a unique opportunity. Nobody else in your market area can make that assertion. The numbers don't lie. So that is both an opportunity and unique to your office.

Being a non-competing broker is another unique opportunity. This is the case for my office. I say to agents, "What that means is I'm available for you anytime. When you need me to pick up my phone, I will. When you need to stop by my office to ask me something, I am available.

My purpose and my responsibility as your broker/owner is to be here when you need me, not off dealing with my own listings and customers." This is something my office has that others do not.

If you are a competing broker, however, you can present that as a unique opportunity as well. You might tell prospects, "That means I'm sharing in the same challenges you are. When you need me, I'm going to know what you need because we are in the same boat, dealing with the same issues. When I learn something because I'm out there prospecting, negotiating, getting listings and working with buyers, I can relate better with you and the situation you're in."

Note that I usually hear the phrase "competing broker" as negative. Instead, I'd use "practicing broker." To me, that completely changes the outlook and the perception for that prospect you're trying to attract into your office.

As you consider unique opportunities, try to come up with an even dozen.

Do you have quality administrative staff? Do you have people who handle all incoming calls? Do they send and receive faxes for you? Do they set up your showings and do all of the things that help you conduct your business?

Do you have an Internet cafe? Do you have an area where agents from other offices and customers and clients can come in, sit down and log onto the Internet to search listings and check e-mails?

What kind of environment does your office have? Is your office paperless?

Do you have a unique brand name? If you're in an a community that has 15 franchises, brand name alone isn't enough. But if that brand name gives you contact management like Lead Street, marketing tools like Design Center, or a J.D. Power and Associates award (or two!), nobody else can claim they have that.

Over time, as you come up with good ideas and find ways to make yourself different, you'll find your competitors copying you. Once it's copied, your opportunity is no longer unique. So some of your unique opportunities must always be changing and evolving.

Remember that imitation is a form of flattery, a sign that your idea was a good one. When your competition rips you off, you need to implement your next good idea. You don't necessarily stop doing what's being copied, you just no longer include it on your list of unique opportunities.

Maybe it's community involvement. In our market, we sponsor our town's big Fourth of July celebration – Red, White and Boom. Nobody else is doing that, so it's a unique opportunity for visibility. But in the future, if we choose not to repeat our sponsorship, somebody else might pick it up. Although it's served us well, it would no longer be a unique opportunity.

Of the dozen unique opportunities you come up with, some will be targets for your competitors to copy. But you should come up with at least four or five solid things that, no matter what, competitors cannot duplicate or replicate.

Our office is at the intersection of the community's two busiest roads. No one can duplicate our location, so that will be a unique opportunity for us for 15 or 20 years.

Questions for YOU:

◆ What are your office's unique opportunities?

Which of your unique opportunities are unlikely to be copied by your competition? Which are likely to be copied?

◆ Of your competition's unique opportunities, which might you be able to copy or neutralize?

◆ What not-yet-existing unique opportunities might you aspire to?

THE SURVEY SAYS?

Cobroker sales are another great source of referrals and candidates for my recruiting hit list.

These are people already doing business with the agents in my office. After a closing, I always send out a survey to my agents asking them to rate the other agent, and whether they would recommend that person to our office.

Let's say I get feedback that the other agent – Carl – was an eight out of 10, that he was very professional, very timely, very courteous and had good communication skills.

That sounds like somebody I'd like to talk to. So I would pick up the phone and call that agent.

"Hi Carl, this is Yoselyn with RE/MAX Realty Team. You had a closing with one of my agents on 2213 Southwest Third Avenue. Can I ask you a couple of questions about my agent's performance?"

I explain that I'm the broker owner and I'm doing quality control to make sure that not only are we exceeding the expectations of our customers, but also the agents we work with in the industry.

So I ask for an overall rating of my agent's performance. Carl tells me she was professional, she had good control of her parties in the transaction, and a whole list of things he liked about her. And I am agreeing with him and starting a little conversation with him.

After a bit, I tell him I don't want to take too much more of his time but that I do have two more questions.

"Are you interested in what my agent said about your performance?" And I tell him about all the good things she had to say about Carl's professionalism, courtesy and communication.

"She gave you an overall rating of eight out of 10." We might talk about that for a moment. "And she said that in order for you to be a 10, you'd have to be with our office. Have you ever considered that?"

That usually gets a little chuckle. But if there's any hint of a positive answer to that question, I ask for an appointment.

"I'd really like the opportunity to talk with you about what makes our office different, what resources we have to help your business reach new levels. I have Tuesday and Thursday available; would morning or afternoon be better?"

If they're interested, they'll set the appointment; if they're not, they won't. And it's one of the easiest, non-threatening ways of getting a candidate in for an interview.

I generally only talk to those agents that my people rate seven or above. But I don't ignore those that get sixes or below. It might be that the agent is just missing something in their office. They might need additional support. So I frequently ask my agents, if someone with a marginal rating were given the environment and the culture and the training we have, might they go from a six to seven or eight? And often, my agents agree that if we gave the candidates the opportunity to work with our people, they would become better agents.

Questions for YOU:

◆ What reasons might you have for contact with competing agents?

◆ What, if anything, would make an effort like this difficult? How might you eliminate the obstacle?

◆ What other aspects of your business might benefit from a survey of performance?

JUST POPPING BY

Another tool for identifying possible recruits is by what I call pop-bys. I spend nearly a quarter of my time on these. Pop-bys are management-by-walking-around. I walk the office hallways and pop by my agents' offices. I make the hallway circuit every morning, every afternoon and right before I leave for the day, so I have three opportunities to reach out to and hear from every one of my agents.

Each time I pop by, I try to make some sort of connection: How's it going? How are you? How can I help? What's going on? What are some of your challenges or frustrations? What's happening with your kids? How was your wife's Christmas party? I try to let them know that I genuinely care about them because I really do. There's a reason I asked them to join the company.

I also ask about competing agents. "I know you're dealing with a couple of agents right now. I think you've got a couple of pendings. If you could think of two agents that you'd like to see here in this office, who would they be?"

My agents are used to the question and frequently have names ready for me. "Tell me a little bit about them. What makes them so good? Why do you want them here?"

What I'm listening for is comments that the competing agents are very professional. They're at work early in the morning and available on the phone. They understand this business. They have great listings. They're just good, strong, solid, consistent agents.

Those are the agents I want to go after. My agents have already given me their names. I go to my office and close my door. I call those agents to let them know the wonderful compliments just shared with me and how my agents want them working in this office and how I think they might be a be a good fit here.

And I ask for an appointment.

Remember that real estate statistics show that nearly half of all agents stay in an office or move to an office because of the broker. They have to like you, respect you, and want to do business with you, both before they become your agent and after they become your agent. You need to build a personal relationship with them. Pop-bys are a way of maintaining that relationship while you're gathering names to recruit.

Questions for YOU:

◆ What means do you already employ for keeping "in touch" with your team?

◆ Are your team members aware of the important role they play in identifying potential recruits?

◆ Is there anything that might stand in the way of an agent's referral? If so, how might you eliminate the obstacle?

TURNING UP THE HEAT

I don't understand why so many people are afraid of the phone. The person on the other end can't reach through the earpiece and slap you or give you a spanking. The worst they can do is hang up. Likewise, why so many are so afraid of cold calls on the phone is beyond me. Changing it from a cold call to a warm call can make it easier.

That's one thing that my co-broker survey and my pop-by question about competing agents have in common: they turn cold calls into warm calls.

You're calling these competing agents to pay them a compliment. "My agent says you're very professional (or thorough, or knowledgeable, or organized – whatever came out of your agent's comments)." They're going to be so tickled, they're going to listen to whatever you have to say because you've just put them – and probably yourself – at ease.

Maybe you won't get an appointment the first time you

call. But if that agent is regularly closing business with your agents, you'll be making a steady flow of calls to them with the co-broker survey. And if that agent is good one, you'll be calling regularly as a result of your pop-by referrals. One day, on one of those calls, you'll hear in their voice that something has changed: they're unhappy or they're dissatisfied.

This is why you make the calls after every closing and every pop-by. You've strategically positioned yourself: you've already let recruits know your agents think highly of them. And you've told them you think they'd be right for your office or have asked to meet with them to see what kind of fit there might be.

Now that something's amiss in their universe, you can almost hear them hoping you'll ask again.

And that makes for the warmest kind of call: one that results in both an interview and, very likely, a successful recruit.

Questions for YOU:

◆ What other opportunities for "warm calls" exists in your office or market?

◆ What other ways can you make multiple contacts with potential recruits?

◆ Would you limit the number of contacts you have with a potential recruit? Why?

FEELING BOARD?

Another area for recruiting efforts is at Board of Realtors events. But you need to be very careful with these, because in many areas – mine included – the Board has a strict no-recruiting policy.

Just because there's zero tolerance for recruiting, however, doesn't mean there's zero opportunity.

People who see me out in public might not know who I am, but they have absolutely no doubt about where I work. I'm wearing a RE/MAX shirt, carrying a RE/MAX bag and pulling a RE/MAX cooler.

I am not a secret agent. I'm a RE/MAX agent, and I am proud to be one. This goes for whether I'm at the gym, in an airport, in a restaurant, or at Board of Realtors functions.

So if I am at a Board event – even though I am NOT recruiting – there will be people attracted by that who will ask for my business card or ask how I like it at RE/MAX.

As I was I walking in to a Board event last year, another broker squared off with me and said, "Do not approach or talk to anyone at this table. This table is all mine." I looked back at her and said, "Okay." What that broker failed to realize is that by telling me not to do something, she really challenged me to find a way to get it done.

This event was a series of classes during which the instructors asked questions about the market. Every time a question was asked, my hand went up. "Who can tell me how many single-family homes were sold last month?" I could: 318. "Who knows what the average list price was?" I did: $141,000. When they asked about average sales price and number of days on the market, I raised my hand because I knew the answer.

Why did I know the answer when many did not? Because I am a source of information for my agents. So I research my market, and I know the trends of the market. I do this daily, weekly and monthly. So when these types of questions were asked, guess whose hand always went up? RE/MAX girl. RE/MAX girl. RE/MAX girl.

So not only am I obviously a RE/MAX agent, but I also obviously know a lot about real estate in our area. That combination of a successful company and market knowledge made me very popular at that event. At every break, I'd end up entertaining a small group of agents who had questions. One agent in particular was practically glued to my side. At each break he'd run over to ask me questions – questions that became more and more about RE/MAX. When he asked for my business card, I gladly gave him one.

After the class was over, I got a phone call from the Board of Realtors. The representative said, "I hate to make this phone call, but it was brought to my attention that you were recruiting during the class, and you know we have zero tolerance for recruiting."

She went on for a while and when she was finished, I asked if I might respond. I very calmly said, "I intend to continue to taking classes at the Board of Realtors. That's not going to stop. Another thing that will not stop is people who ask me for my business card will get one. And if they ask me questions about RE/MAX or about my office, I will answer them. I will also wear RE/MAX clothes and carry RE/MAX gear because I'm damn proud to have that balloon."

There was silence from the other end of the call which I know she was uncomfortable making in the first place.

"One more thing," I said, "You might want to call the broker who complained and let them know I have a meeting with their agent Monday afternoon."

A meeting, I might add, that was arranged well after the board event, but that was entirely a result of the interest the agent developed during the event.

Here's the key. I don't solicit at board events. Agents seek me out, and if they do, by golly, watch out. That's how passionate I am about who I work with, what I work for, and what I stand for.

Questions for YOU:

◆ What is your Board of Realtors' policy on recruiting (don't take someone's word for it; it's likely written somewhere)?

◆ If you're prohibited from recruiting at Board events, what can you do?

◆ How can you use visibility at Board events to your advantage without violating policies?

FINDING THE TRUTH IN STATISTICS

P eople who work in college admissions have it figured out: if you need to rank a lot of people in a short time, use their numbers. For college admissions, those numbers are test scores – SATs and ACTs. Students' "numbers" give a good indication of how they'll perform academically at college.

When I first started recruiting in Florida, I had a universe of about 6,000 local agents. To decide which ones I wanted on my hit list (mainly because I didn't have any better ideas), I went to their numbers in the Multiple Listing Service. While delving into MLS statistics represents only a small portion of my recruiting time now, it was how I spent most of my time in the beginning.

When I use MLS statistics today, I look at an agent's production level ($2 million and over is a nice break point). I note how long they've been in the business (I like to see two years or more). And I like to see that they have a decent book of business: listings and pending sales.

Although the MLS was set up as a tool for agents, the agents' information also makes MLS a great tool for brokers, owners and recruiters.

And while "the numbers" might not tell an agent's whole story (there are some with lower sales or less experience that I'd love to have on the team, and some with higher sales and vast experience that I'd avoid under any circumstances), like college test scores, they can provide a quick indicator of who you should consider setting your sights on.

Questions for YOU:

◆ In addition to production levels, what other numbers might help identify potential recruits?

◆ Where, other than MLS, might you find numbers to help identify potential recruits?

◆ What important factors might not show up in MLS? How might you find them?

WHEN THEY PAY
TO REACH YOU

You can also find prospects in the newspaper. Right there between the ads for new cars and appliances.

I keep an eye out for agents who run their own ads in the paper (or on TV). To me, this means they have a budget for advertising and an entrepreneurial mindset. Agents who advertise likely already understand budgeting and business planning.

These are important factors in an agent embracing the RE/MAX system. For some recruits, it's a real challenge to grasp; for someone who's already budgeting and planning their business, the RE/MAX system is second nature.

Watching agent ads also gives me an opportunity to talk to agents that I didn't turn up with my other efforts. This only gets a small part of my recruiting time now, but it's a great way to find agents that I might have otherwise missed.

Questions for YOU:

◆ What publications can you watch for agent advertising?

◆ What other agent activities demonstrate an agent's business savvy? How can you watch for these activities?

◆ As a recruiter, through what activities would potential recruits know about you?

POSTCARDS:
WISH YOU WERE HERE

After the telephone, my other means of staying in touch with the potential recruits on my hit list is postcards.

Even though the phone is my primary tool for contacting prospective recruits, I only call when it's appropriate and necessary. I call to congratulate them on a successful year or an accomplishment. I call them if we've had any co-brokered sales. I call if I see them at a networking event. But I never call them just for the sake of calling them.

I like postcards because in addition to reaching my hit list, they also get me inside agents' homes. That means my message gets across to their families.

Whoever gets the mail, whether it's their spouse or their kids, everyone is going to see it. And if the agent comes home upset with their broker, their spouse or their kids might say, "Why don't you just go to RE/MAX? They keep sending you all this stuff." And the agent might say, "Maybe

I should give Yoselyn a call." So postcards help put families on my recruiting team.

Every month or so, I send the agents on my hit list a postcard. It's not always about the office. It might be a Valentine's Day wish, it could be Thanksgiving, it might be about a class we're doing where anybody can come and learn.

My postcards are another way to get my message out, they get in front of families and are regular reminders to an agent that I am still interested.

So when a tension develops in an agent's broker/owner relationship, they've either recently received a postcard from me, or they're about to.

Questions for YOU:

◆ In what other ways might you stay in touch with agents on your hit list?

◆ What other means of reaching agents might also reach their families?

◆ What is the longest period someone on your hit list could go without a contact from you?

THE COLDEST OF CALLS

Sometimes, no matter how much you try to warm up a call, the chill remains. And when it does, it simply means the agent isn't ready and you need to move on.

When agents – especially good ones – get a call from the broker or the owner of an office, they know who you are. And if you do any degree of recruiting, they might put their guard up: "Oh, it's Yoselyn again. She's going to try to sell me on RE/MAX."

So sometimes when you call, you'll sense agents aren't open to your call. Or perhaps they're just busy. Maybe they picked up the phone only because they didn't recognize your number. For whatever reason, they're preoccupied.

That's okay. You can tell when somebody wants to talk to you. It doesn't have to be anything specific that they say or do, you can just feel it. Likewise, you can feel it when there's no connection.

In much the same way that you can tell when someone

is smiling on the other end of a phone call, you can sense when someone isn't.

And that's probably the best way to gauge your next step. If you sense that person you've called is smiling, go for it. Ask for the appointment.

But if it seems like they're having a pissy day, just thank them for their time. If you were calling about a co-brokered sale, thank them for their part in it. Let them know if there's anything you might do to help them sell more real estate, you're right down the street. And say goodbye.

Sometimes you'll get abrupt answers to your questions. Just "yes" or "no." You need to get off the phone as quickly as you can and recognize that it's not directed at you. The timing is just wrong.

Remember, you're not trying to sell them anything. So just gauge by the conversation on the phone whether or not you'll ask for an appointment. If you don't think they're open or warm enough or they seem a little guarded, end the call and live to recruit another day.

Questions for YOU:

◆ If a potential recruit seems guarded on one call, what might enable you to get through that guard on a future call?

◆ If you decide to cut a call short, under what pretense might you check in another time?

◆ Would you ever ask candidates the reason for their apparent reluctance?

NUMBERS NEVER LIE

Like most tasks in sales, recruiting is a numbers game. As your selection process improves and your interview prowess grows, the numbers get a little easier. But it never stops being about the numbers.

Let's say you'd like to add one agent to your office. In the early days of recruiting, you might have a closing ratio of one in five. So you need five interviews for one close. To get one interview might take 10 calls, so five interviews needs 50 calls, or five days of 10 calls each day.

It's just like prospecting when you're trying to list a property. You want to fill up your pipeline. You are constantly prospecting and farming because you know you want closings in January and February. Hell, if you're not preparing for those closings in November and December, you just have to work twice as hard come March and April. But if you fill the pipeline enough, something is eventually going to happen on the other end.

My office sees 100 or more sales a month. So the co-broker survey alone is good for 20 or 30 calls a week. Add in some referrals from my agents and other sources and there are plenty of agents to call. You just have to remember to make the numbers. Every day.

Some people need a visual for remembering to make those calls. Early on, I committed to make 10 calls every day. I had a shot glass filled with 10 gold coins. Every day, I'd dump the coins into a pile on my desk. Then, for every phone call that I made, for every person that I talked to, I dropped a coin back into the glass. Even with my door closed, my office manager and then-broker could hear the clinking and knew I was making progress toward my goal. And the little pile of coins kept me focused on what I still had left to do. So if you need a visual reminder or a physical process, get a little glass and put some quarters in it.

From now on, make these calls an everyday activity. I recommend getting them out of the way first thing in the morning so you don't have to worry about forgetting (or putting it off). If for some reason you're unable to make your calls – maybe you're sick or go on vacation – the next day or the next week, you have to make up what you missed.

Because recruiting is a numbers game and you have a pipeline to fill.

Questions for YOU:

◆ If you're already recruiting, what is your closing ratio? If you haven't begun, what do you expect it to be?

◆ How many calls would the co-broke survey generate in your office?

◆ In addition to the co-broke survey, and based on your closing ratio, how many calls would you need to make in order to meet your recruiting goal?

THE DECIDING FACTOR

I n my experience, there are two types of decision-makers in the world: emotional and logical. Knowing which type your prospect favors (and which type you are) is critical to the recruiting process.

From the first handshake in my office, I'm determining whether you're an emotional or a logical decision-maker. If I shake your hand and you're an emotional type, you're going to have a strong, sturdy handshake, but your eyes are going to be smiling. Your face is going to be animated. Your body language is going to be relaxed. There's going to be genuine warmth coming off from you.

If, on the other hand, you are a logical type, you're going to have a very strong, firm handshake, but very little smiling, very limited facial animation, very little sense of warmth.

It's not that either of these decision-making styles is good or bad or better or worse, it's just that prospects needs something very different depending on which style they favor. And it's your job to give it to them.

When you're dealing with an emotional decision-maker, your interviews will require more time because you're going to be jumping from family to vacations – it's going to be more personal. I saw a picture of a baby on a prospect's iPad. I asked about it. That led to a discussion about the woman's son, which morphed into a conversation about her dog.

What you're really looking for with the emotional decision-maker is things you have in common.

When an agent's phone rang during an interview, I asked if she needed to take the call. "No, it's just my daughter," she said. "I'll call her back." I asked how old the daughter was. She was in high school. "Which school?" I asked. Turned out to be the same school my son is in. "Does she play any sports?" I asked. She was a cheerleader. "Really? My son is on the football team." And the connection is made.

With an emotional decision-maker, the conversation goes in every direction, because an emotional decision-maker has to feel love around them, comfort, joy, happiness. They need to have it warm and fuzzy.

An analytical person could give a hoot about the warm and fuzzy, they don't care. They're there for one thing and one thing only: "What can you do for me? Show me the numbers. Show me how I can make more in less time."

Both types want the same thing. It's just that their motivations are very different, so they need it presented a different way. With that analytical logical decision-maker, interviews are usually much shorter: 45 minutes tops. If that person glances at their watch, you're done. Give them the facts. They love charts, statistics, and graphs. So if you have a nice compact presentation ready for them, you're golden.

Questions for YOU:

◆ What kind of a decision-maker are you?

◆ In what ways can you modify your natural style in order to "mirror" a prospect?

◆ Why might a blend of decision-making styles amongst your team be desirable?

CONCENTRATE YOUR EFFORT

had worked for Century 21 back in Boston and had applied for jobs at two Century 21 offices here (though neither of them returned my call). When I started recruiting for my RE/MAX office, care to take a wild guess who was the first agency I set my sights on?

If you're picturing a target with Century 21 in the bullseye, you've got it.

I zeroed in on Century 21 because I understood them; I had been there before and recruited agents into their system. Since they're corporately owned, they don't change much from one brokerage to another. I knew what agents had been told in order to get them on board, and I knew what frustrations they felt once they started.

I started looking at local office numbers and their agents' statistics and made a list of all the agents I wanted to talk to.

In my market we have more than 4,000 agents; it's a large market. It was way too many to consider for recruiting and for being able to pick and choose who I wanted to talk to. By narrowing the list to those who worked for specific offices, I had a manageable target.

A large universe of prospects by itself is not a good thing. Volume is only a benefit when you find a way to concentrate your efforts.

Questions for YOU:

◆ By what parameters could you focus your recruiting efforts?

◆ Could you benefit from a focus on an office? A franchise? A geographic area?

◆ Is there a focus you should avoid?

TEN DAYS OF HELL

While recruiting can create opportunities for your office, it can also create problems for your competition. And those problems can create even more opportunities for you.

As I bring on new agents, their absence is felt at the office they are leaving. The top producers, the middle producers and the bottom producers all feel it. I make waves in that office that can create a lot of uncertainty among the agents and make that office vulnerable to a recruiting attack.

When I take an agent from another office, I find that the office is vulnerable for at least 10 days following the agent's departure. That's prime time for me to go in there and really pick and choose who I want to come to my office.

Somebody is leaving. There's chaos, gossip and rumor. Agents manifest their own uncertainties about the office: I bet she left because the manager took her leads... I bet she left because she did not get her sign calls. What they are really doing is validating all the reasons they should be leaving, too. As a recruiter, I just need to listen to what they are saying, recognize what it is, and zero in my efforts on it.

For those 10 days, the brokers are be beside themselves because they don't understand what happened. Morale dips because the whole office is questioning why somebody would leave. Our office is perfect; what's going on? They are vulnerable, and that is prime time to go in and attack.

Something I learned in my first year: When your competition is drowning, shove a hose down their throat. It's not personal; it's business.

I know it's better in the long run for an agent to be with my office – especially a professional agent who understands the business, wants to succeed and reach new levels. If I didn't feel so passionate about it, I wouldn't be able to attack. But because I do feel that way, when there's a vulnerable office, I need to go in there and clean house. For the sake of the agents, I need to close offices down, because I truly care about them. They need to be with my office, and in the long run they'll be better, more successful agents. Overall, it's better for everybody.

I can say with certainty that there has been no time in my career, with thousands of agents, where I have had remorse or regret over taking somebody from an office.

This is why I always ask for recommendations and referrals when I'm interviewing an agent. Each new contact in an office is like planting seeds for tomorrow. Every phone call you make is just planting a seed. Every interaction you have with another agent is just planting a seed.

And every time one of those seeds grows up and leaves to become a new agent in my office, a new period of vulnerability begins for a competitor.

Questions for YOU:

◆ What would happen in your office if you lost a good agent to a competitor? How would your team react? How would you react?

◆ How might you take advantage of an office's uncertainty when someone other than you landed the first recruit?

◆ How could you adjust your hit list and recruiting calls to take advantage of an office's uncertainty?

WHEN AT FIRST YOU DON'T RECRUIT, TRY, TRY AGAIN

As you get names from your office's co-brokered sales and your own office pop-bys, many agents' names will come up more than once. It's inevitable that a successful agent will co-broker multiple sales with your office. And if agents are any good, more than one of your team will mention their names.

The temptation is to say to yourself, "I don't need to call them for the co-broke survey. We just did one a couple of weeks ago."

Resist temptation: call them every time.

I can't force the time to be right for that agent. There's nothing I can say or do. But by talking to them on a consistent basis, I form a relationship and assure that I'm in the picture when the right time comes.

All I'm waiting for is something to happen in their office. And I want to make sure I'm who they think of first when that something happens. That when I make what I think is going to be a routine repeat call, they say, "Hey, Yoselyn, I want to schedule that appointment. Can we get together? Can we talk?"

Most recruiting isn't overnight. It isn't instant. Some might come together faster than others, but most, you need to cultivate over time.

Especially in the case of the co-broker survey, even if I've spoken to the agents recently, I still want to know how my agents performed. And even if the agents aren't going to meet with me, I still want them to have the opportunity of hearing how they rated with my people.

By making my calls every time their name comes 'round, I'm making sure I'm in position whenever their circumstances change and the time becomes right for a move.

Questions for YOU:

◆ In what ways might you sense a potential recruit is ready for an overture?

◆ How easily could you be reached if a potential recruit wanted to speak with you?

◆ What are other ways you might remain in front of potential recruits over time?

SETTING THE STAGE
(OR STAGING THE SET)

By the time candidates come for an interview, we might've spoken on the phone a dozen or more times. There were likely numerous co-broker surveys and several referrals from pop-bys to my agents' offices. I might have also found reasons to call with congratulations for some of their accomplishments.

Hopefully, I have gone a long way toward "becoming their broker before I'm their broker."

Now is NOT the time to make a poor impression.

The moment those prospects walk into my lobby, my administrators greet them by name (if they don't already know their names, I make sure to let them know who I'm interviewing and why). "Hi Steve. Yoselyn's waiting for you. Can I get you something to drink? I'll give her a call right now. She'll be out in just a moment."

When I bring them back to my office, they see my very

nice executive desk. But that's not where I'm headed. Instead of sitting behind the desk, I always sit in front of it, along with my prospects. They're already stepping in to my lion's den. The last thing I want is some sort of superior-inferior setting.

I put our chairs close enough together that I could reach over and touch them. I'm trying to show we're on the same level for this conversation.

I've also already printed or gathered any materials I think I might need for the interview. And I've checked and double-checked anything I'm planning to show on my computer.

This is the show. And it's about to begin.

Questions for YOU:

◆ What could you do to improve the environment for an interview in your office?

◆ What materials might you develop for potential recruits?

◆ How might you make a potential recruit feel more comfortable about your meeting?

WHAT TO EXPECT WHEN YOU'RE EXPECTING AN INTERVIEW

n the beginning, the only thing I knew about how I was going to conduct interviews, was how I WASN'T going to conduct interviews. I WASN'T going to talk and talk and talk and tell the candidate everything I knew, when I didn't know whether they wanted to know it.

After hundreds (or thousands?) of interviews, I have refined a method that has repeated success.

I begin by setting my expectations for the interview.

"I'd like to ask some questions to get to know you a little bit better, to hear what you've been doing, what your aspirations are and what systems you're using. I'm also going to introduce RE/MAX to you so we can determine whether you're a good fit for RE/MAX and whether

117

RE/MAX is a good fit for you."

"If the fit is good," I say, "I'm going to ask you to join."

The candidates are likely nervous, so I want to put them at ease. But I also want to prepare them, because if I feel there is a match, I am going to them ask them to join. By openly setting this expectation (and with their consent), I've taken the scary part away from what we're about to talk about.

Sometimes I hear that they're not ready to make a decision today. I tell them, that's fine, but whether they make the decision tomorrow, next month or next year, I want to know today, whether RE/MAX is a good fit for them, and vice versa.

The key to all this is they know what to expect: at the end of the interview, they're going to know if it's a good fit for them. And if I think they're a good fit, I'm going to ask them to join.

Nothing scary or intimidating about it.

Questions for YOU:

◆ What other expectations of the interview could you share with a potential recruit?

◆ What expectations might the candidate have of the interview?

◆ How might you help a potential recruit see a match with your office?

PINPOINT THE PAIN

The real estate world is flooded with acronyms: REO and FSBO, MLS and HOA. And here's a new one to use when you're interviewing a candidate: PAIN. Which helps you remember what you need to pinpoint from the agent's point of view:

P is for their Personality (or decision-making style).

A is for their Anguish (more on this in just a moment).

I is for their Interests.

N is for their Needs.

During your interview, you'll take these out of sequence. You'll start with the P for Personality, as you need to know right away whether you're dealing with an emotional decision-maker or a logical decision-maker. Your reading of this factor will determine whether you need to dish up a just-the-facts presentation or a warm-and-fuzzy one.

Then, you'll jump to the I for Interests and begin asking questions that help you learn more about the candidate in a non-threatening way. Try to stay on the positives: what they like, what they like to do, what got them into the business, their greatest successes, what they're most proud of. You'll pick up some tidbits, but for the most part, this is just calming conversation.

After a period with their Interests, it's time to start probing the A for Anguish. There is a reason they've agreed to meet with you. A reason that is both real and important to them. You must pinpoint what that reason is by asking the right questions.

Listen for responses like these:

"My broker is out there listing and selling properties. The other day, I needed him because I had this deal that was going sideways, but he didn't return my call."

"Our office recruiter just brought on a bunch of new agents, so now all the training sessions are geared toward getting the newbies up and running. There's nothing for me."

"I've been a consistent producer for years. But the new agents get all the up-calls and the walk-ins."

"I stopped taking up-calls and walk-ins because it's more of a pain in the ass than they're worth. If I can't make it because I have another buyer or seller to meet, I have to find another person who will take my time, and I have to get it okayed by my broker or my manager before I can let this person take it over."

Through statements like these they identify their Anguish. Often, it's so insignificant you'll want to laugh. They're willing to make a major move to your office because they have to get a swap approved? Because newbies have cut into their training time? Because a busy broker didn't return their call right away?

Realize that their Anguish is rarely just one thing, it's

an accumulation. It's needing to get a swap okayed AND diminished training time AND an unreturned call AND the absent congratulations after five new listings...

But sometimes all you'll hear about is that they discovered the office ladies room has changed from two-ply to one-ply toilet paper. The heartless inhumanity! The hurt and anger they display as they relate this snub is very real. But before you start worrying about what you have on hand in your restrooms, remember that the toilet paper is NOT the whole story – it's just the straw that broke the camel's backside (or at least rubbed it the wrong way).

Through this process, you'll also identify the N for Needs of your prospect. These aren't usually as volatile or emotional as the Anguishes, but they, too, will be an important part of the steps to come.

As the Anguishes and Needs become clearer, you'll be tempted to pounce on the candidate's negative situations and solve their problems. Don't. It's not yet time for that. Just make a note of them and mentally file them away for later.

Questions for YOU:

◆ Can you see the benefit in delaying the solutions?

◆ What might a member of your team identify as an "Anguish" in your office?

◆ Should you be concerned about the "little things" accumulating in your office?

◆ Are there offices in your market where the "little things" have been piling up?

QUESTIONS
ARE THE ANSWER

n all of my interviews, I ask a lot of questions. And they're very different, depending on the type of candidate I'm with. And I always know what to ask because I write the questions down. I always write open-ended questions, because the answer to one question will lead to another, and those answers provide different directions to explore. "Help me understand this... what kind of policies do you have? What kind of management support do you get? What else does your office offer?" Questions like these get and keep candidates talking.

Early on, I like to ask them to tell me about their office and its culture, what attracted them to that office and what they like about it. Inevitably, they begin by talking about how wonderful it is and how much they love the people. And I find ways to agree with – or at least acknowledge – most everything they say.

That usually leads to the "buts": I really like this, but... I am very happy, but... the policies are great, but... There is always a "but," a reason why they are meeting with me. I just need to identify what that reason is, and I do it through what they tell me.

After we get to the "buts," I ask, "If there were things that you could change in your office, what would they be?" or "If you were going to start your own office, what would be important to provide for your agents?" If it hasn't already, this is when it all comes out.

If the interview is an hour and a half, I spend a good 45 minutes asking questions. There are times when we veer completely off course talk and about their kids or the vacation they just took or the football game; it's perfectly okay, because I am establishing rapport and relationship.

Certainly, this is a business transaction, but you cannot lose sight of the personal side. Not only do they have to like you and respect you and want to do business with you, but it's a two-way street. You must get emotionally attached to the people you work with, because you spend the majority of your time with them. You see them every day, and you need to establish that culture in your office with people who share the same values you do.

Along with the personal side, I'm listening for hints about their dissatisfaction. It might be policies, lack of structure, lack of systems, lack of management support. It might be that their broker is a competing broker, that there is no support system, that there is no training, no lead generation... the list goes on and on.

While you're getting comfortable with the interview process, it's a good idea to have some of your questions written down. You might not use every question on your list every time, but if you ever draw a blank, a list of questions can be a life-saver.

Can you tell me a little bit about how you do business?

How do you prospect?

Do you farm?

How would you describe the culture in your office?

Can you tell me a little bit about your database and how you work it?

What's the structure of your office?

Can you tell me about the training programs in your office?

What about opportunity time in your office?"

While these topics might seem benign, they will likely cause prospects to identify their own pain.

Questions for YOU:

◆ What are some questions that would help you determine a potential recruit's...

Anguish?

Interests?

Needs?

YOUR CONFIRMATION NUMBER

When prospects begin identifying their PAIN (especially their Anguish and Needs), it's very near time to offer solutions to their problems (as we've been taught to do since we started in sales). But I've found there is a very important, intermediate step: confirmation – especially if the PAIN aligns with one or more of your office's unique advantages.

For example, let's say that their "everything is great, but..." is that they're provided no system for managing their contacts. I'll ask them, "If there were a system provided to take care of that for you, would that be something you would find valuable?"

And that's all I say.

Then, I'll ask them how much time they're spending on contacts, now. They customize all their brochures and their "just listed" and their "just sold" and they do a newsletter... I get them to tell me that it probably takes a good day to get all of the articles and the information. And then they have to put it together...

I make sure I understand what they tell me they are lacking, but I don't offer a solution. I'm checking to make sure that this is a problem they would like to solve. But there's no need to start solving problems yet. We're just identifying – and confirming – the ones that need solving.

I don't offer solutions yet, because I still want them to tell me more. So I say, "Let me see if I understand you correctly..." and then I repeat what they've said.

I ask, "If there was a system where all you have to do is pick out the layout, and all the information is given to you, and you could do it in one hour instead of eight, would you appreciate seven extra hours for listing, selling, prospecting, calling, negotiating? Isn't the best and the highest use of your time, in front of people?"

And then I ask, "If we have this system in place, would that be something that would be interesting to you?"

I still don't get into the selling phase here; I'm just teasing the feature a little, and confirming what I'll need to come back to.

Questions for YOU:

◆ Can you envision a problem which a candidate would not be interested in solving?

◆ How might you help candidates prioritize their problems?

◆ How might this technique be used in other processes in your office?

SELECTING
THE SOLUTIONS

After all this preparation, it's finally time to introduce solutions to your prospect's PAIN.

Here's where you take what you've noted and confirmed and offer your solutions. But you will ONLY offer solutions to the problems that have been discovered and confirmed. You will ONLY talk about what your prospect mentioned as Anguishes, Interests and Needs, aided by your office's unique advantages.

If fees were not raised as an issue, do not mention fees. If they don't bring up training, workshops or office meetings, don't talk about them. If you do, you'll lose them. By addressing only the things that are important to them, you will make them feel good. You've dived deep into their problems; now you're building them back up again. When they leave your office, you want them to be on a high.

"You mentioned that up-calls are more of a pain than

they're worth. Let me explain how we handle our up-calls and our walk-ins..."

"You mentioned that your broker wasn't available when you had a deal that was going sideways. I'm a non-competing broker so I'm always available. I have an open door policy. And if I'm not in my office, I've got my cell phone on me. I'm just a phone call, a text message or an e-mail away. The only time I won't answer is if my door is closed and I'm with another agent and I want to give him my undivided attention. Because I'm not out there with sellers and buyers and negotiating deals, you can almost always reach me. And if I'm not in the building, I have back ups who are as good as me..."

"You mentioned you would like some kind of system to help you reach out to your database on a regular basis. I'd like to show you our Lead Street software..."

This is where you introduce those solutions. This is where you put a name to your quality administrative staff, your office systems, your status as a non-competing broker (or a practicing one).

But ONLY in those places where the prospect has asked for help through Anguish, Interests and Needs that you have identified and confirmed.

It's interesting to note that rarely is money the issue here. Money doesn't come up because money alone is rarely the problem. Agents want an office, a culture and an environment where they're going to be happy (and where the emotional decision-makers will get their warm and fuzzies). They want to feel welcome and embraced. Money comes from being productive. In the right environment, they know they'll be productive. They're going to kick ass and take names.

Questions for YOU:

◆ Are your office's unique opportunities likely to align with prospective recruits' Anguish and Needs? If not can you develop and explore some that will?

◆ Might you use this part of the interview to identify areas for creating unique opportunities in your office?

◆ How would you proceed if none of a candidate's Anguishes or Needs could be solved or met by your office's unique opportunities?

IT'S NOT ABOUT
LOVE OR MONEY

Much as prospects' complaints about their offices are rarely about one thing, questions they have about money are rarely about money alone. Instead, a question about money usually relates to the ease or difficulty of earning it.

And because you've already asked your probing questions to identify your prospect's PAIN, you should already know where to track back to.

"How many listings do you have out there? Ten?

"Do you purchase your own signs, or does the office provide them for you?

"Since the office provides them, that means the office phone number is on that sign. How many deals have you missed out on because you didn't have your phone number on that sign and you didn't get the buyers?

"Well, with a $3,000 average commission, if you've missed

two, that's $6,000, right?

"So having the freedom to put your own number on your signs could be worth an easy six grand a year? And with more listings and a better commission structure, couldn't it be even more?

"In my office, you make the investment of buying your own signs, but you generate all the calls as a result of it. No more missing deals because somebody's on floor time answering the office phone calls."

The key to money questions is to put a tangible value on your solutions to them. Sometimes it's about a policy that lets them make more money. Other times it's a solution that saves them time. These tangible values are especially beneficial for a logical decision-maker. This is where they buzz in.

The same principle holds true for the "love" problem: "I can't leave because I love my broker."

The problem is not love for the broker. It is an uncertainty over what candidates will say when they quit. Anyone expressing this problem is asking you, "Can you tell me what to say so that I cause a minimum of hurt feelings and still get to join, here?"

Likewise with the "listings" problem: "I can't leave because I have too many listings right now."

The problem is not too many listings. It is an uncertainty over knowing how to handle listings during a change of agency. Anyone expressing this problem is asking you, "What is the best way to handle the listings that I have as I make my move to your agency?"

Often times, these questions will come up just because the prospect feels that questions are expected of them. Don't attach more importance to the questions than the questions deserve. Stick to the PAIN you've identified.

Although the patient presents with a complaint of one thing, the diagnosis usually reveals that to be a symptom of a different problem in their current situation – a problem revealed by your careful questioning in the interview.

Questions for YOU:

◆ What other complaints about one thing might actually be about another?

◆ What other problems can you put a dollar value on? What other solutions?

◆ What is the danger in solving a stated problem instead of solving the problem at its root?

THE CLOSE

In old, traditional sales models, all the energy, all the attention, and all the training went to the close. In the newer model I recommend, the close is almost an afterthought. In the old style, it was the foundation of the pyramid; in this style, closing is the tiny top of the pyramid with good strong interviewing at its base.

Think about the process:

You used pop-by agent referrals and co-broker sales surveys to have conversations with likely candidates.

You asked those candidates to meet with you about the possibility of joining your office. You likely asked them several times: this time, they agreed.

At the beginning of the interview, you set an expectation: "If I feel you're a good fit for my office, I'm going to ask you to join."

Then, you spent a long time determining whether they'd be a good fit, uncovered some PAIN in their current situation, and demonstrated solutions that might make your office a better fit for them.

You opened the door to any questions they might have for you.

Everything you've done has been leading to the final question. Which is actually two:

"Do you have any more questions for me? If not, I have one question for you: can you see yourself as a RE/MAX agent?"

If they say yes, I say, "Let's go find your office."

If they say no, I know the timing isn't right and I'm likely to hear from them when it is.

That's all there is to the close. Because the sale was made through everything that led up to it.

Questions for YOU:

◆ How different is this closing process from the one you presently use?

◆ What are the advantages of the shift in balance (more qualifying, less closing)? What are the disadvantages?

◆ Are there other processes in your office where a similar effort might be employed?

ONE AND DONE

One of the most common reasons agents won't join an office (and one of the most stupid on the office's side) is because the agent was never asked. Even after they were identified, accepted a meeting and were interviewed, they were never asked to join the office.

Often, they get trapped in an endless string of interviews.

I know of broker/owners and recruiters who do three and four interviews with prospects. That's crazy. I intend to get my prospects on the first – and only – interview.

To me, repeat appointments would be a terrible waste of time. They would take me away from first appointments with new prospects that would put me closer to a new agent. Meeting the same agent again and again would not be the best or the highest use of my time. I'd rather work my process, make my numbers, and get it done the first time.

When asking an agent to join is as simple as asking

whether could they see themselves as a RE/MAX agent, I can't fathom leaving that unasked after an interview shows a candidate to be a good fit.

I might get together again for lunch, but that's only because I can tell I already have them on board. They just need to be asked again.

And then, we can pick their office.

Questions for YOU:

◆ What are the benefits of fewer meetings with potential recruits? What are the drawbacks?

◆ What might be a reason to have a second or third meeting with a given candidate?

◆ How can you ensure you remember to ask "the question" in every qualified interview?

GETTING PAST MAYBE

A friend of mine says that his two favorite answers are "yes" and "no"; his least favorite answers are "maybe" or "I'm not sure."

With a yes or no, you know how to proceed. With a maybe/I'm not sure, you don't.

When I ask a prospect if they could see themselves as a RE/MAX agent, I do NOT want to hear, "I need to talk it over with my spouse." That is a maybe/I'm not sure of the first degree.

When I hear it (and it comes up often), my internal voice – which I manage to keep quiet – says, "That's a load of crap!"

How many of us would contemplate a life-altering decision without including our significant others in advance? How miniscule is the likelihood that this prospect's spouse is blissfully unaware of the meeting with me?

Load. Of. Crap.

If they were thinking of buying a car, they'd talk about it ahead of time. "I'm going to stop by a dealership next week.

I'm going to take a test drive." If they were thinking about a computer, it'd come up in advance: "My computer is a little slow; I'm thinking about a new one."

Making a career move from one organization to another is not going to go unmentioned. And it likely has been a subject for many conversations already.

So the spouse knows exactly where they are. Their kids probably know exactly where they are. The whole family is waiting for the call from the office parking lot to find out how the meeting went.

My response (this one, in my external voice): "What's your spouse's name?"

And I pick up my phone.

"Let's call and share the good news!"

Which they won't do. But they realize they've been smoked out.

Another way of avoiding this particular "maybe" is to suggest in advance that the spouse or partner accompany the candidate to the interview.

Otherwise, when I get a "maybe" or "I'm not sure," this is not yet a "yes." But it is also not a "no."

So I start talking to them like they're already here.

I'll handle all the paperwork for the state and the board; what's your full name?

I'm going to give you a termination letter; should it be dated today or tomorrow?

I'm going to give you a 'Please Release my Listings' letter; what are your active listings?

Do you want pictures on your signs?

Do you list your cell phone number or direct line?

Do you want your website on your signs?"

Any answers to those questions mean "yes." And like my friend, that is one of my favorite answers.

Questions for YOU:

◆ What are other ways to nudge indecision into a yes or no?

◆ What are the advantages or disadvantages to getting a clear, definite answer.

◆ What are other ways a candidate might express maybe/I'm not sure?

FIT IS A
TWO-WAY STREET

The closing question of whether prospects could see themselves as RE/MAX agents rarely gets a "no" from the agents.

But sometimes it does from me.

Remember the expectations for the interview: for the agents to see whether we'd be a good fit for them and for me to see whether they'd be a good fit for us.

I will not ask them to join unless I think they would be a good fit.

There are times where the agent says, "I want to join," but I feel they are not a good fit.

It is difficult to tell an agent I've just spent an hour or two interviewing, "You know what, I don't think now is a good time for you to join our office." But I can't feed them a line of crap. I have to look them in the eyes and tell them.

I make the point to try and be a prospect's broker before I'm their broker; in this case, I have to fire them before I hire them.

When do I realize an agent might be a bad fit?

During the interview, when I asked them to tell me about their business, I heard, "Well I don't prospect, I don't market, I don't do this and I don't do that."

Which makes me wonder what they expect from me, because I am sure as hell not going to give them business on a platter. I can't care more about their business than they do.

Or they've said, "I take a listing, but then I don't talk to the seller until closing because I don't like people. I don't like talking to them. I don't like picking up the phone."

Well I'm not going to field those calls for them. The last thing I want is to have to deal with is someone else's upset buyers, upset sellers and upset agents.

I do not want these people in my office. And I am not going to ask them to join.

But because 75 percent of my conversations are with prospects that either my agents or I have pre-approved, I rarely end up wasting my time with this kind of "bad fits." Not only are my agent pop-bys and co-broker surveys a good source of names, they are source of quality names.

Those pre-qualified leads let me work more efficiently and more effectively, and keep me away from the agents I have to say "no" to.

Questions for YOU:

◆ What might tip you off to a bad fit with a prospective agent?

◆ What might you learn from recruiting mistakes you've made?

◆ Are there instances in which the same recruit might be a good fit at one time but a bad fit another time?

WHEN THE FIT
GOES BAD

Early in my recruiting interviews, I manage expectations by letting candidates know that if I think there's a fit, I'm going to ask them to join.

There is also an important corollary for down the road: if I think there is no longer a fit, I will ask them to leave.

Telling someone they need to leave the team is definitely one of the my least favorite things to do. But sometimes it is necessary.

It should never, however, be a surprise.

When I find myself questioning the fit, I put agents on a probation period. This forces me to articulate the problems I'm seeing and ensures the agent is reading the same page. I call them into my office and I outline what they are doing and what they are not doing. If they've been paying attention, the meeting doesn't come as a surprise. It just confirms there is a problem and gets it out in the open.

I always come out of a probation meeting with an agreement on specific, measurable goals. We'll agree that they'll do a specific number of deals before the quarter is over and how they're going to do it. I hold them accountable. I make sure it's a situation where if they do everything they say they're going to do, then the result will be closings. If they don't have the closings, it will be because they haven't done what they said they would.

During the probation period, we'll talk many times about how they're doing toward their goal and how I might help.

At the end of the probation period, we'll both know how things went, so there's no surprise.

Many times, the probation period, the discussion about performance and the plan for improvement are all that's needed to get an agent back on track.

Sometimes, however, it simply identifies a problem the agent is unwilling or unable to remedy.

Despite the unpleasantness, when you ask an agent to leave, it can actually build morale in your office. The other agents know who is failing to pull their own weight. If you keep agents like that on the team, the other agents – the ones who are busting their butts and doing what needs to be done on a daily basis – take notice. They say, "She's going to bring on anybody and she's going to keep anybody just for the sake of doing it." So when you let someone go – although it's difficult and you genuinely care for that person – you are doing the entire office a favor. It shows the other agents you appreciate what they do. It's something that has to be done for the greater good.

And often, you're doing the agent a favor by simply saying, "This is not a good fit at this time."

Questions for YOU:

◆ Have you ever kept someone on your team longer than you should have? To what result?

◆ Are some production or performance problems easier solved by early attention?

◆ Under what circumstances, if any, would you keep a poor-performing agent on the team?

RETENTION: RECRUITING THE ONES YOU ALREADY HAVE

With all the attention and effort given to recruiting new agents, it is important to note that retaining existing agents is even more important. Fortunately, the process is identical.

My definition of retention is recruiting the agents I already have. So I continue doing the things I did to bring them on board. I give constant, "How are you?", "That's a great job," "'Atta boy" and "'Atta girl."

I maintain an active interest in their business and how I might help. I regularly ask what they need or what they need me to do. When I pop-by their office, it's not just to get names of potential recruits. I want to know how they're doing, what their kids are up to. I show I am sincerely interested on both a personal and professional level.

Just like with a potential recruit, I'm always asking about areas for improvement. What are some of their frustrations and how can I help? What are some challenges they're experiencing in the market? Sometimes, the problems are the same ones I use to attract agents here: a need for systems, more leads, better support. And often, the solutions I offer are the same: Have you considered doing this for lead generations? Have you thought about this type of system to help you with your showings?

I am always trying to identify new ways to make their workload easier, and they appreciate my effort. Regardless of whether a given solution eventually works, they know I tried and they know I have an active interest in helping them achieve their goals. Most times, it's just a matter of showing them I care.

From a recruiting standpoint, you want to be their broker before you're their broker. But from a retention standpoint, you must make sure you still act as their broker after you're their broker.

Questions for YOU:

◆ Which members of your team are most vulnerable to a recruiting effort? What can you do to protect them?

◆ How might you stay in better touch with your team members?

◆ What tools or services might you provide to help team members achieve their goals?

PERSPECTIVE
ON THE TOP

've learned to be very quiet about what I think someone should earn. It is far more important to concentrate on what they think they should earn.

If an agent wants to make $500,000, that is their goal. If I can help them go from $300,000 to $500,000 both they and I would say they are top producers. If someone else is making $50,000 a year and I can help them make $70,000, they, too, are top producers.

Some people are content and pay all their bills and spend time with their families and do a good book of business under a $100,000 year. They are top producers in their family and their own line of business.

Others are freaked out because they didn't make $500,000 last year.

Every agent is different. And every agent has their own idea of income success. It's my job to help them increase their business next year, whether it's an extra two deals during the year or an extra two deals a month.

Questions for YOU:

◆ In what ways might an agent might determine "success"?

◆ What advantage might your office gain from production diversity among your agents?

◆ When an agent uses a different criteria for success than you do, how can you help them meet or exceed their goals?

AFTERWORD:

LOOKING AHEAD

After reading this, I hope you view recruiting in a new and different light.

I hope you are no longer intimidated by the word "recruiter" or "headhunter."

I hope you see that recruiting really just boils down to building relationships. And that we are in a relationship business.

Recruiting is not rocket science. It's the simplest, easiest thing you can do.

I hope you see that there isn't anything difficult or unusual in what I do. I just make it a point to do what's simple, every single day.

Yes, there are times when the last thing I want to do is pick up the phone and call people. But I have learned the critical importance of doing it and getting it out of the way. When it's done – and only when it's done – I can spend the rest of the day concentrating on things that are more attractive to me.

I hope you see that recruiting is not as hard or as difficult or as unappealing as people make it out to be.

If you are passionate about your business, if you are passionate about the company you work with, why not tell that to everybody who is willing to listen?

It's what I do. And I hope you will, too.

ABOUT THE AUTHORS

Yoselyn Hollow is broker/owner of RE/MAX Realty Team in Cape Coral, Florida. In 2011, she was recognized by RE/MAX, LLC as the "Top Recruiter in the Nation." In 2010, REMAX/LLC named hers, "Outstanding Brokerage of the Year," and gave an "Office Volume Award" for more than $200,000,000 in business. She lives in Cape Coral with her husband, Michael, and two children.

You can reach Yoselyn at yoselynh@remax.net

Kevin Pierce is a writer and voiceover artist in Fort Myers, Florida. He writes and produces "The Florida Environment" radio program, broadcast on Florida's public radio stations. He hosts a television interview program about development of Florida Gulf Coast University. And he collaborates on training, education and marketing projects for clients around the world. He lives in Fort Myers with wife, Cindy, and two children.

You can reach Kevin at kevin@kevinpierce.com

64585229R00104

Made in the USA
Lexington, KY
13 June 2017